THE
CAFÉ DES ARTISTES
COOKBOOK

Detail from Spring.

THE
CAFÉ DES ARTISTES
COOKBOOK

BY GEORGE LANG

FOREWORD BY BRENDAN GILL

PHOTOGRAPHS BY MICK HALES

Clarkson N. Potter, Inc./Publishers

Published by Clarkson N. Potter, Inc., 201 East 50th Street, New York,
New York 10022. Member of the Crown Publishing Group.

Manufactured in Hong Kong

Design by Gael Towey Dillon, with George Lang

Library of Congress Cataloging in Publication Data
Lang, George
The Café des artistes cookbook.
1. Cookery, International.   2. Café des Artistes
(New York, N.Y.)   3. New York (N.Y.)—Restaurants.
1. Title.
TX725.A1L26   1984   641.5'09747'1   84-15041
ISBN 0-517-55307-4
10 9 8 7 6 5 4

NOTED WITH GRATITUDE

Too many cooks not only spoil the consommé, when they get together on a cookbook the result usually is disastrous. I hope this little volume will serve as an exception, even though at least six people must be acknowledged with gratitude.

Often, admiring a chef and getting to know him is like loving goose liver and then meeting the goose. If you have a chance to meet *André Guillou,* however, the Breton chef emeritus of the Café, you will realize that this extraordinary craftsman is an exception to the above axiom. André's classical training and upbringing in the countryside of France allowed me to implement my vision of a menu with comforting and delicious food. His successor, Executive Chef *Thomas Ferlesch,* who is Austrian-born, has the ideal sensibility and skill to carry the Café's regional European menu into the twenty-first century.

André, Thomas, and *Steve Gurgely,* the Café's director, represent the tradition and excellence of this seventy-five-year-old establishment.

To make sure that someone who has never tasted the dishes will be able to reproduce them, we were fortunate to have *Deborah Mintcheff* retest all the dishes in our private kitchen and clarify steps and instructions.

There are cookbooks that give you great quantities of information, but not the kind you need to make the dishes successfully, and there are scores of volumes that give you just the right *amount* of information, but of the wrong kind. *Donald Jonas* acted as the project manager of this book, making sure that the balance was well kept. His good spirit inspired everyone to complete the manuscript under the trying conditions of a busy restaurant kitchen.

Nancy Novogrod, our perceptive editor, separated the wheat from the chaff and assured the wheat was baked into a good loaf.

George Lang
June 1992

CONTENTS

For Jenifer Harvey Lang
whose inspiration
and virtuoso skill in the kitchen
shaped this little book
in many subtle ways
G. L.

FOREWORD

by BRENDAN GILL

In its early years, New York City was suspicious of artists and writers. Having been founded as a trading post and port, it took care to devote itself to commerce, which is to say to single-minded money-grubbing. The gross and canny Dutch who settled Manhattan island and their usurping successors, the gross and canny British, knew where they were when it came to money; it appears that they thought of little else, except perhaps on Sundays. On Sundays they thought of God, and of how his intercession on their behalf might help to make them even more prosperous than they were.

For generations, New York was notorious for its unbridled pursuit of gold, which had at least one incomparable advantage over the pursuit of aesthetic or spiritual concerns: it was down to earth. Gold could be seized, bitten, and stuffed into mattresses, and it set standards that everybody understood—a man who made a hundred dollars a year was obviously twice as good as a man who made only fifty dollars a year. What Frost was later to sum up as a form of Yankee wisdom was already a commonplace in eighteenth-century New York: "Take care to sell your horse before he dies; the art of life is passing losses on." It was still shrewder, of course, never to suffer any losses at all. Accumulation was a one-way ticket to happiness, or what seemed happiness. The New York proposition was: "I am rich, therefore I can buy anything I wish, therefore I must be happy."

As the years passed, other American cities in their prosperity began to discover that there was more to life than merely piling up fortunes. Boston, Philadelphia, and Baltimore, to say nothing of Newport and Charleston, came to perceive that pleasure was to

1

be found in spending money as well as in acquiring it; having achieved a certain eminence in the world, the mercantile class felt eager to call attention to that eminence and, at the same time, to fill its leisure hours with appropriate avocations. Taking a cue from the Old World, the New World consented to embrace the arts. Timidly at first and then more and more boldly, they became patrons of painters and sculptors and writers and even of the theater (meaning playwrights but not actors and actresses, who were reputed to be of low moral natures).

By the end of the first quarter of the nineteenth century, even the obdurately philistine citizens of New York were ready to make some room in the hurly-burly of their daily lives for the cultivation of things of the mind as well as of the countinghouse. When Dickens came to New York in the 1840s, a number of worthy literary lights were on hand to welcome him. The leader among them, Washington Irving, was hospitable enough to offer Dickens a new American invention—a cocktail—which Dickens pronounced himself delighted with. Alas, history fails to tell us what the cocktail consisted of; it was probably rum.

So artists and writers became an accepted feature of New York, already vehemently on its way to becoming the biggest and richest city in the country. A few of these artists—Thomas Moran, Jasper Cropsey, and Frederic Church, painter of incomparably icy icebergs—earned substantial incomes; the rest lived as they could, in garrets and lofts, in the improvident fashion that has always caused prudent businessmen to regard them with dismay. They tended to be such bad managers, after all; sometimes even when they succeeded, they failed. A painter might earn a great reputation and earn considerable sums along with it and still contrive to die broke, causing his wealthy patrons to shake their heads in contemptuous rebuke. Still, there have always been a few artists as clever about making and keeping and multiplying money as if they were bankers; in our time, we call to mind such artist-tycoons as Warhol, Rauschenberg, Johns, Pepper, and Steinberg, who no doubt can

speak as knowledgeably about puts and calls as any denizen of
Wall Street and who, if they live in a loft, live in a million-dollar
one, owned—like the rest of the building, and maybe the rest of
the block as well—solely by them.

Affluent, practical-minded artists of this kind first gained a
measure of prominence in New York in the late nineteenth century. They worked in handsome, spacious studios in the neighborhood of Washington Square, but they lived in houses or
apartments elsewhere in the city (Chelsea was a favorite residential
district, as was Gramercy Park, and a few brave souls were ven-
turing north to Murray Hill and beyond), and it galled them to be
paying rent in two different places at once. A well-known land-
scape painter named Henry W. Ranger hit on the notion of de-
signing a structure that would combine ample studios with living
quarters for the artists and their families and that, like only a few
other buildings in the city at that period, would be owned on a
cooperative basis by the residents themselves. Ranger took his
notion to a builder named William J. Taylor, who worked out the
financial details and then set about buying a parcel of land suitable
for the experiment. It was just past the turn of the century; the
ever-increasing population of the city was heading rapidly uptown.
The north side of West Sixty-seventh Street struck Taylor and
Ranger as ideal for their purposes; occupied largely by low brown-
stones and stables, land there was still comparatively cheap, and it
had the advantage of being close to Central Park. The two entre-
preneurs called upon the architectural firm of Sturgis & Simonson
to design the building that still stands at Number 27 West Sixty-
seventh Street.

Begun in 1901, the building was ready for occupancy by 1903
and proved an immediate success. The living quarters of most of
the apartments were laid out as duplexes, with ceilings eight to
ten feet high and windows facing south to take advantage of the
sun; the studios were two stories high and had immense windows
facing north, to provide a flood of shadowless light. Many artists

took up residence in Number 27, along with people who, though not artists, were friends of artists and collectors of their works and wished to partake of an ambience that was rather bohemian and yet reassuringly upper-middle-class. "Monkey see, monkey do" is a saying as true in the world of real estate as in any other; Number 33 West Sixty-seventh Street, designed in approximately the same austere neo-Renaissance style as Number 27, by Simonson and his new associates, Pollard and Steinam, was completed in 1905, as were Numbers 15 and 35 (Steinam and Simonson), while Number 39 (Pollard and Steinam) was completed in 1907. It was characteristic of most of the buildings on West Sixty-seventh Street that they were far more romantic-seeming within than without. It was also characteristic of their architects that they kept changing partners, in a sort of game of musical chairs that had less to do with temperamental or artistic differences than with where the financing of a given building happened to come from. Number 1 West Sixty-seventh Street, the first building in from the corner of Central Park West, was an exception to the rule of exterior austerity; its carved stone trim and castlelike fenestration hinted at centuries-old acts of derring-do. Designed by Pollard, it was begun in 1915 and completed a couple of years later. Though grandly entitled the Hotel des Artistes, it was never a proper hotel. On its ground floor was, and is, and, one hopes, always will be, the celebrated Café des Artistes. The apartments above it were intentionally without kitchens; one telephoned down to the Café for one's meals, which were sent up by dumbwaiter. The idea was to be able to dine well without a cook in residence. The system soon broke down, but the Café, open to the public, flourished from the start.

A busy decade and a half of construction on West Sixty-seventh Street! The celerity of the changes was, of course, characteristic of New York; their nature can be judged by some vivid scraps of recollection set down by the artist James Montgomery Flagg, whose apartment in Number 33 later belonged to the distinguished art collectors Louise and Walter Arensberg and belongs today to

||||||||||||||||||||||||||||||||||||||||||||||||||||||||||||||||||||||||||||||||||||||||||||||||||||||||||||||||||||||||||||||||||||||||||||||||||||||||||||||||||||||||

George Lang, owner of the Café des Artistes and author of the very book that the reader holds in his or her hands. Looking back on 1903, Flagg wrote, "There never was such a street in town as West 67th: fine, modern apartment houses on the north side and, on the south, stables; disreputable [brownstone] tenements; a garage that burned up three times; and on the corner a notorious saloon, which kept the night raucous with female yells, stabbings, and bums hurtling out onto the icy pavements in wintertime."

As the years passed, the number of famous (and in some cases infamous) people who came to dwell on that single short side street is difficult to credit—in our imagination, its sidewalks begin to be as crammed with readily recognizable faces as some vast mural caricature by Hirshfeld, in which we are able to tick off, one after another, dozens of the most written-about figures of our dwindling twentieth century: Isadora Duncan, Noel Coward, Rudolph Valentino, Zasu Pitts, Jo Davidson, Alla Nazimova, Alexander Woollcott, Fannie Hurst, Lawrence Tibbett, Marcel Duchamp, Al Jolson, Philippe Halsman, Mae Murray, William Powell, Childe Hassam, Heywood Broun, Paul Whiteman, Edna Ferber, Ludwig Bemelmans, Ben Hecht, Roy Chapman Andrews, Robert Lowell, Guy Bolton, Elizabeth Hardwick, John Lindsay, Norman Rockwell, Maurice Maeterlinck . . . Given such a cast of characters, how many scenes, violent and tender, must have been played out in those big paneled studios, by firelight and moonlight!

Many of the personages noted above lived, for periods short or long, at the Hotel des Artistes. Two particularly violent scenes took place there in the fateful year of 1929. Time darkens all things; it also romanticizes them, and the writer Peter Salwen has given a welcomely colorful account of events that must have filled West Sixty-seventh Street with horror and dismay:

On the afternoon of January 13th, Renee Fuchs let
herself in to her brother's top-floor studio. Emil Fuchs had

Detail from Spring.

Detail from Spring.

been court painter to Queen Victoria and Edward VII, and he suited the popular idea of the "fine" artist: tall and gentle, with white hair and beard, a soft felt hat, and voluminous black bow tie. A bachelor, he maintained his sister in the Endicott Hotel on Columbus Avenue, from where she came daily to prepare his lunch. But when she arrived that quiet Sunday she found him dead, seated in an armchair on the balcony overlooking the studio.

Aging, his work out of fashion, Fuchs had known for some time he was dying of cancer. That noon, he had dressed carefully, brushed his hair and beard, donned the silk sash with his medals on it, and arranged the portraits of his royal patrons in a semi-circle facing the balcony. Then he ascended the steps, settled himself in a Sheraton armchair, and gazed at the faces of his former friends and patrons as he sipped a vintage port that had been given to him by Victoria. He spent a few minutes writing a short note to his sister. Then, using a small hand mirror to locate his heart, he shot himself. The weapon was a tiny pearl-handled revolver, inscribed "To Emil Fuchs from Edward, Prince of Wales."

Salwen goes on to describe the deaths of Harry Crosby and his lover Josie Rotch, in the studio of the painter Stanley Mortimer, a close friend of Crosby's:

Crosby, 31, was a favorite nephew of J. P. Morgan and a scion of one of Boston's most patrician Back Bay families, and had been one of the more romantic literary figures of the Twenties: poet, publisher (his Black Sun Press in Paris had published Hart Crane, James Joyce, and D. H. Lawrence), gambler and opium devotee, he wore a black cloth flower in his buttonhole and liked to organize somewhat ritualistic orgies. On the afternoon of December 10th, while Crosby's wife and mother were waiting for him to appear for tea at Uncle Jack's Madison Avenue townhouse, he and Josie had borrowed Mortimer's place for what their host assumed was a routine tryst. But when Mortimer forced his way back into the apartment that night, after getting no answer to his knock, he found them in bed, barefoot but otherwise fully dressed, and innocently holding hands. Harry's right hand, draped around his lover's neck, gripped a .25-calibre revolver. Each had a bullet hole in the temple.

It would be hard to picture anyone less like poor Crosby in social position and temperament than the most renowned artist living in the Hotel des Artistes in 1929. This was Howard Chandler Christy, who had been born in a log cabin in Muskingum County, Ohio, in 1873, studied under William Merritt Chase, and disgusted Chase by giving up "serious" art in favor of becoming one of the most sought after magazine and book illustrators in the country. Christy was a friend and rival of Charles Dana Gibson, whose ubiquitous "Gibson Girl" set the standard for beauty among American women in the early 1900s. Soon the "Christy Girl" was setting a somewhat similar standard, though it must be noted that where the Gibson Girl was passionate but chaste, the Christy Girl was openly flirtatious; she was coarser and more carnal, and these differences were manifested by the artists themselves. Gibson was aristocratic and monogamous, Christy earthy and hard-drinking; it appears that he found it as natural to sleep with his models as to draw them, and a host of friends of both sexes reveled in the jovial rowdiness of his mind and person. In the twenties, he gave up magazine illustration for formal portraiture; among the dignitaries who sat for him were Warren G. Harding, Herbert Hoover, William Randolph Hearst, and Benito Mussolini. Between 1940 and his death, in 1952, he devoted himself to painting large historical canvases; his masterpiece in this genre is *The Signing of the Constitution of the United States,* which hangs over the grand staircase of the Capitol, in Washington, D.C. Whatever its other distinctions may be, it is said to be one of the largest canvases ever painted in the United States, measuring twenty by thirty feet.

A portrait of Howard Chandler Christy,
by James Montgomery Flagg,
hangs behind a table near the bar, above.
Etched glass lighting illuminates the bar, right.

In 1932, the board of directors of the Hotel des Artistes proposed that the appearance of the Café in that grim depression year might be much enhanced (and business consequently much increased) by the painting of murals on the Café's walls. There were at least thirty-six artists living in the building at the time, and it was expected that each of them would be willing to contribute a single work, but during the next year the artists quarreled so bitterly over the question of who was to paint which mural where that the board decided at last to turn the entire task over to Christy. He painted a total of thirty-six pert nudes in a variety of seductive but not very naughty poses, counting on an abundance of foliage, feathers, and falling water to conceal what Adam and Eve, egged on by an angry Jehovah, grew unaccountably ashamed of as they made their sorry way out of Eden. The nudes have been described as reflecting "the artist's splendid sense of design, and the use of color and form," and that may well be the case; what matters more to us is that they do honor to his randy old evergreen heart. The Café is a happier place for the relish with which he carried out the commission of the board of directors; his pinkly silken hamadryads instruct us by their wanton rompings in how far we have come from those dour Dutch burghers and buttoned-up Britishers of the seventeenth century.

We are lucky to visit here on West Sixty-seventh Street, to find ourselves among artists and writers whom their fellow New Yorkers regard not with suspicion but with adulation. Along with actors, actresses, and athletes, they have come to be counted among the most cherished of our local folk heroes. Seated in this snug Café, we raise a glass to them and to the merry ghosts that crowd about us, saints and sinners alike. Noel Coward (surely in black tie) is one such ghost, and we can scarcely do better than to quote a toast that the father of the family speaks in Coward's charming *Cavalcade:* "To ourselves, to each other, and to the happiness of us all!"

AN AFFECTIONATE INTRODUCTION

No one really knows the history of the first twenty-five years of the Café des Artistes, but at least I'm able to write about its last two decades with some authority.

In the spring of 1975, I received a phone call from media consultant Dave Garth, representing the board of directors of the Hotel des Artistes on my block in New York. He asked me if I would be interested in taking over the Café. As an answer, I quoted Mark Twain's line about the man who was to be tarred, feathered, and ridden out of town: "If it weren't for the honor, I'd rather walk."

Being quite satisfied with my little think-tank which develops restaurants and retail complexes around the world for other people, I did not want to go back into operations in an era of steady disintegration of workmanship, especially with a dark, dingy little restaurant at the entrance to an apartment house that was empty most of the time—this despite the fact that Lincoln Center was already over a decade old.

A couple of nights later, it was raining and, as usual, no taxis were available. I said to my wife, "If I had a successful restaurant on this block, we would always find a taxi." The next day I called my board member friend and, without having gone through the careful feasibility studies that should precede such decisions, I blithely told him: "I'll take it."

A month or so after this a local paper ran the headline: CAFE DES ARTISTES PACKING ITS PAINTINGS TO LEAVE CO-OP . . . The lead continued: ". . . Landmark will be closing. The Café des Artistes at 1 West 67th Street is shutting its doors for the last time on May 31st [1975]."

Detail from Swing Girls.

Parrot Girl.

The papers had a field day with the battle that ensued between the former lessees, who claimed they owned the paintings, and the co-op (with me in the middle). The final outcome, negotiated by our lawyers, was announced by another paper on July 8 of the same year: THE NUDES WILL STAY ON CAFE'S WALLS.

I recently recalled that my late uncle, a noted physician, would not operate on any of his relatives: "The emotional involvement decreases your competence," he used to say. That's how I felt after creating and opening several hundred restaurants for others and finally being faced with one of my own. As I usually do when I have to reckon with the future, I took another look at the past, especially because I knew that none of today's formats would be the right solution.

A very important part of the heritage of the Café des Artistes is the fact that artists lived and worked in virtually all of the buildings on our block. They were a highly colorful and social group, whose activities—based on a recently found costume and documents—even included the selection of the first Miss America, Edith Hyde, at the Chu Chin Chow Ball at the Hotel des Artistes in 1919 (Howard Chandler Christy and James Montgomery Flagg were among the prominent artists who served as judges). The Café was a meeting place between creative efforts, offering reasonably priced food flavored with good conversation; and it also served an essential function for residents of the Hotel des Artistes. Because the sumptuous duplexes had only tiny pullman kitchens, the famed tenants bought their own raw ingredients, sent them down to the kitchen of the Café des Artistes with instructions for cooking, and the kitchen then sent dinners upstairs on dumbwaiters precisely at the time requested. To keep cold foods in the pantries of the apartments a Rube Goldberg–like twenty-ton ice machine, in the basement, circulated frigid icewater into each apartment's icebox.

My present office at Number 33, which used to be connected with a glass and cast-iron corridor to Number 27, served for a couple of decades beginning in 1905 as a small restaurant-club for the artists in these buildings. Both this little place and the Café were fashioned after the English ordinary, a cozy bistro with a limited menu based on foods available at the market. The genre was introduced to New York by a Mr. Thomas Lepper in the mid-eighteenth century. While the bistros of France, trattorias of Italy, beisls of Vienna, and tavernas of Greece—all equivalents of the ordinary—flourish to this day, the style never became popular in the United States.

Tradition is often just a form of conspiracy to keep the future from happening, but adapting this old-fashioned concept to the current market served the Café well. The menu categories are based on foods ranging from seafood and veal to complex tortes and frozen desserts, and our chef only fills in any of the categories if the ingredients are available in prime condition on that particular day. It wasn't a lofty grande cuisine I was aspiring to create, nor its many strange and faddish offshoots, but a cuisine with the flavor and texture of a neighborhood restaurant where good middle-class food, typical French Sunday dinners, would be rounded out by some "If only I could have" type dishes.

Anyone who knows his or her onions when trying to style a restaurant makes a list of self-imposed rules that may in equal parts reflect the contributions of a carefully conducted market study, a divining rod, and intuition. My goal, which I believe has been successfully realized, was to re-create the warmth of a middle-European coffeehouse restaurant that is occasionally left by the habitués for such necessities as brief and dutiful visits to their homes before hastily returning to their *stammtisch,* their steady tables.

My philosophy was to make all the improvements in such a way that even the guests who had frequented the restaurant for decades would not notice drastic alterations. Walls and murals were moved to enlarge the main dining room by ten feet; seating arrangements, color schemes, lighting, floor levels, kitchen layout and equipment

The central buffet table holds a selection of desserts, above.
Flowering plants bloom in the windows by one of the restaurant's
most popular tables, left. *Detail from* Fall.

—just about everything was changed. Heavy drapes had blocked out the daylight and the connection with the street; these were removed. Murals were liberated from a quarter-inch of soot and grime and lit properly for the first time since they had been painted by the famed Howard Chandler Christy.

I decided to keep the entire staff and, through motivation and instruction, create a team that would have the skill of their European counterparts. The major exception was Stephen Gurgely, the Hungarian-born and Italian- and American-educated Director of the Café, who joined us just before the opening. With André Guillou, the Breton-born chef who had worked at the Café for twenty years by that time, Steve and I launched a series of tastings during the first four months of my ownership. (These tastings still take place a couple of times a month and, for this little volume, they were simply intensified to daily events in order to avoid the Homeric perils of nontested recipes.) We also concentrated on developing personalized specialties of the house, our "thumbprint" dishes, some of which you'll find in this book.

My concept excluded foods that are the characteristic symbols of elegance or expense accounts (often synonymous these days) like truffles, imported foie gras, caviar, or broiled beef. I was determined to introduce honest dishes of the *cuisine bourgeois;* to pay special attention to "mother-love" items—foods like bread, butter, coffee, or brewed tea served in double pots; we make our own chutneys, smoke our own fish and seafood, prepare an enormous variety of traditional charcuteries, and offer a large selection of fresh fruits. Our menu does not include dishes that are based on ingredients less than noteworthy in the United States (like roast veal or roast pork), and bars all fried foods, which I didn't feel belonged at the Café.

Serving Peach Melba or a purchased fruit tart seemed to me out of place at the Café, yet, within the mazelike spaces of the restaurant located on two levels—one subterranean, the other slightly below ground—I was not able to set up a pastry shop.

This troubled me until I one day realized the simple solution: the neighbors should bake for a neighborhood restaurant!

A sample scene from the last few years: A Very Important Person from a major corporation is talking about his monumental project in our consulting office (which has nothing to do with the Café); suddenly my secretary announces that two ladies are outside with four cakes. The meeting is immediately suspended, plates and forks are brought out, and everyone becomes an instant dessert expert.

Such experiments eventually resulted in a stable of about a dozen people, both male and female, who create desserts at home, making their own specialties or using dessert recipes we give them, as well as about the same number of tiny one-pastry-chef shops doing the same. But before we got to this sweet state, we tasted enough Sacher tortes to sink the Austro-Hungarian Empire.

The world is full of would-be wine connoisseurs who are waiting for the opportunity to say: "This is a withered wine with discipline and forceful finesse, but . . ." (and they pause here for effect) ". . . it is also fierce and succulent." The world of restaurants is also full of meaningless wine lists that complicate the simple pleasures of choosing a wine. At the Café, we offer several wine baskets, the kind in which the wines are brought up from the cellar, each containing a changing array of French or California red and white wines, all for the same modest price.

Although brunch has existed for at least seventy-five years, most probably as a late or second breakfast, a *déjeuner à la fourchette,* it only became popular in the United States in the early 1960s. As project director for the Tower Suite on top of the Time-Life Building in New York City, which was opened in the winter of 1960, I was part of this brunch revolution—we used to serve five to six hundred elegant five-course brunches every Sunday.

By 1975, it was time to bring brunches out of the "If it's Sunday noon, it must be Bloody Mary and omelette" syndrome, and Sat-

urday and Sunday—the days when it used to be closed—the Café became, according to local gossip, the place to drink the best apricot sour, spread your marrow (accompanying the pot-au-feu) on your toast, have your Smoked Salmon Benedict, read the out-of-town papers, and celebrate the fact that you were spending the weekend in the greatest city in the world.

In an era long past, Fannie Hurst, Maurice Maeterlinck, Isadora Duncan, Alexander Woollcott, and Mayor Fiorello LaGuardia had their regular tables at the Café. Now it's filled every day of the week by Paul Newman, Rudolph Nureyev, Kathleen Turner, James Levine, Beverly Sills, Isaac Stern, Itzhak Perlman, Alec Baldwin, television stars, top magazine and newspaper editors, Parisian chefs, restaurateurs from all over the world, and anyone who is passionate about good conversation, honest wine, and food that satisfies.

A few years ago we decided to share some of the latter with our friends by publishing a selection of our recipes.

Traditionally, cookbooks were compendiums of recipes that the author had personally perfected through years of experience, and the resulting little bound volumes were passed down through the generations from mother to daughter. The following recipes culled from the Café's large repertoire are not necessarily original creations. This is a designation that is only used by loose-talking amateurs and professionals who are not familiar enough with the work that has gone before them, but these recipes do amount to a passionate guide to the Café des Artistes experience.

On occasion, when I pass by the small portrait of Howard Chandler Christy (done by his friend James Montgomery Flagg)—who was known to be a connoisseur of good wine and beautiful women—I hope that gazing around from behind table number 38, at the back of the bar, he is as pleased by it all as I am.

A view of the restaurant with Spring *in the background,* overleaf.

APERITIF

PEAR CHAMPAGNE

*A*long with caviar and truffles, champagne connotes elegance. Lucius Beebe, the late, great journalist, reported on the gustatory and social glamour of drinking champagne concoctions in the 1920s, when the smart set first discovered them. The following champagne cocktail made its debut at the Café in the fall of 1977, when I served it to a pear-loving friend.

¼ cup sugar
1 slice fresh ginger, the size of a quarter
1 fresh Bartlett, Anjou, or Comice pear, peeled
*   and cored*
2 tablespoons Williams pear brandy
*   Dry champagne*

1. In a saucepan, combine sugar, ½ cup water, and ginger, and bring to a boil. Place the pear upright in the liquid. Cover and simmer until almost cooked. The fruit should remain slightly crunchy.

2. Quarter the pear and place each quarter upright in a separate champagne glass. Divide pear brandy among the glasses and fill with champagne. Serve immediately.

SERVES 4

APPETIZERS

CLAMS ON THE HALF SHELL, MEXICAINE

 3 tablespoons finely diced onion
 2 tablespoons finely diced red pepper
 2 tablespoons finely diced green pepper
 2 tablespoons finely diced red ripe tomato
 1 teaspoon minced garlic
 ½ teaspoon cayenne pepper
 6 tablespoons olive oil
 2 tablespoons fresh lemon juice
   Salt to taste
24 extra small littleneck clams, washed and well
   chilled
 2 lemons, cut in half crosswise

1. In a small bowl, combine all ingredients except salt, clams, and lemons. Cover with plastic wrap and refrigerate overnight. Season mixture to taste with salt when ready to use.

2. Just before serving, open clams with a clam knife and leave on the half shell. Top each clam with approximately 1 teaspoon relish.

3. Spread a layer of crushed ice on four plates and arrange six clams on each, placing a lemon half in the center. Serve at once.

SERVES 4

ASPARAGUS WITH TWO DIPPING SAUCES

O ne must have the grace to control one's enjoyment of magnificently fattening foods, but asparagus is light and healthful and can be eaten in great quantities without serious consequences. The egg yolk instead of hollandaise makes the dish even lighter. The fact that asparagus is a finger food makes this recipe possible.

1 ½ *pounds large asparagus spears of approximately uniform size with tightly closed tips, rinsed and drained*
½ *cup melted butter*
4 *large eggs*
Coarse salt and freshly ground black pepper
2 *lengths of butcher's twine*

1. Cut off the woody ends of the asparagus spears. Peel each spear downward from just below the tip, using a vegetable peeler or paring knife.

2. Divide asparagus spears into two bunches.

3. Stand one bunch of asparagus on end, with tips facing down, making sure all tips are even and touching the work surface, and taking care not to break them. Using a length of butcher's twine, tie each bunch securely in the middle.

4. Using a sharp knife, trim the bottom of the bunch by cutting through the stalks, in a single stroke if you can manage it, so the stalks are all the same length. Repeat steps 3 and 4 with the remaining asparagus.

5. Bring an 8-quart pot filled with 7 quarts of salted water to a rapid boil. Lower the asparagus bunches into the water. After the water returns to a boil, cook, uncovered, for approximately 3 to 5 minutes, or until stalks are tender, but not soft, when pricked with a fork.

6. While asparagus is cooking, cook butter in a small saucepan over medium high heat for 3 to 5 minutes, until it takes on a nutty brown color. Do not burn. Keep warm.

7. At the same time, cook eggs for 3 minutes in boiling salted water. Remove from water.

8. Lift the bunches from the water by slipping a kitchen fork under the twine. Drain well. Cut twine with scissors and discard.

9. Arrange asparagus on a preheated platter lined with a cloth napkin dipped into the asparagus cooking water to absorb drips.

10. Put soft-boiled eggs in egg cups and cut off the tops of their shells.

11. Divide brown butter among four small ramekins.

12. Serve asparagus at once with salt and pepper on the side. Stalks are dipped into eggs and brown butter separately.

SERVES 4

SALMON GRAVLAX
WITH MUSTARD-DILL SAUCE

|||||||||||||||||||||||||||||||||||||||||||||||||||||||||||||||||||||||||||||||||||||||||||||||||||||||||||||||||||||||||||||||||||||||||||||||||||

For best results, use only very fresh salmon. As an extra garnish, slice salmon skin into thin shreds and fry till crisp in a mixture of vegetable oil and butter; sprinkle on the gravlax at serving time. The same recipe can be applied to whitefish, king mackerel, salmon trout, and other oily fish suitable for marination.

 2 pounds fresh center-cut salmon, bones removed and skin left on, cut in half crosswise

 2 tablespoons aquavit

 ⅓ cup kosher salt

 ⅓ cup sugar

 2 tablespoons freshly crushed (not ground) black peppercorns

 ¼ pound fresh dill

MUSTARD-DILL SAUCE

 1½ tablespoons white wine vinegar

 1¾ tablespoons granulated sugar

 ½ cup olive oil

 5 to 6 tablespoons prepared Dijon mustard

 1 tablespoon chopped fresh dill

 1 heaping tablespoon freshly ground white pepper

GARNISH:

 10 sprigs of dill

 5 lemons, cut in half crosswise

1. Wipe salmon fillet dry with paper towels. Place one half of salmon fillet on top of the other, and trim so that they are even in length. Sprinkle each half of fillet with 1 tablespoon of aquavit.

2. Combine salt, sugar, and crushed pepper, and rub some of this mixture into each half of the fillet without skin.

3. Put half of the fillet, skin side down, in a baking dish. Evenly distribute the ¼ pound dill over the fillet. Cover with the other fillet half, skin side up. Sprinkle the remaining salt mixture over the top. Cover with foil.

4. Place a large platter or chopping board over the fillets and weight with a brick. Put in the refrigerator and let marinate for at least 24 to 36 hours, turning the salmon fillets over together every 12 hours.

5. While the salmon is marinating, prepare mustard-dill sauce by whisking vinegar and sugar together in a small mixing bowl until sugar is dissolved. Slowly add olive oil, whisking well until all of the oil is incorporated. Blend in mustard and chopped dill, and season with white pepper. Cover and refrigerate until needed.

6. After salmon has finished marinating, remove foil and dill. Using a stiff pastry brush, remove all of the seasoning mixture.

7. When ready to serve, slice the salmon very thin on the bias. Put four or five slices on each serving plate. Ladle a small portion of mustard-dill sauce alongside and garnish with a sprig of dill. With each plate serve a lemon half.

SERVES 10

HOT CHICKEN LIVER MOUSSE
WITH TARRAGON SAUCE

||||||||||||||||||||||||||||||||||||||||||||||||||||||||||||||||||||||||||||||||||||||||||||||||||||||||||||||||||||

A dinner appetizer or a luncheon main course of surprising lightness, this recipe is based on the recollected taste, or memory, of a similar preparation created by the late giant of a chef, Albert Stockli of the Four Seasons Restaurant in New York.

CHICKEN LIVER MOUSSE

¾ *pound chicken livers, soaked in water in the refrigerator overnight*

2 *eggs*

1 *egg white*

2 *tablespoons finely chopped shallots*

1 *teaspoon finely chopped garlic*

Pinch of dried thyme

Pinch of freshly grated nutmeg

Salt and freshly ground black pepper

¼ *cup heavy cream*

TARRAGON SAUCE

1 *tablespoon finely chopped shallots*

5 *tablespoons unsalted butter*

⅓ *cup dry white wine*

2 *tablespoons finely chopped fresh tarragon*

1 *cup heavy cream*

Salt and freshly ground white pepper

1. Preheat the oven to 375°F.

2. To make the mousse, rinse chicken livers under cold running water; drain well. Pat dry with paper towels.

3. Purée all mousse ingredients except cream in a food processor or blender, scraping down the sides of the bowl or jar several times. The mixture should be very smooth. Gradually add the cream, blending well.

4. Pour mixture into four well-buttered 6-ounce ramekins or other ovenproof dishes. Place in a shallow baking pan. Add enough hot water to come halfway up the sides of the molds. Bake for 25 to 30 minutes, until mousse is set and a knife inserted in the center comes out clean.

5. To make the sauce, sauté shallots in 3 tablespoons butter in a small saucepan until translucent, about 2 to 3 minutes. Add wine and tarragon. Reduce over medium high heat until liquid is almost evaporated.

6. Add cream and cook for about 6 minutes, until slightly thickened. Remove from heat and whisk in the remaining 2 tablespoons butter, a tablespoon at a time, to finish the sauce. Season with salt and pepper. Keep warm.

7. To serve, gently run a small knife around the sides of the mousse to loosen. Invert onto warm serving plates. Top each mousse with a portion of sauce and serve.

SERVES 4 AS APPETIZER

SNAILS WITH PROSCIUTTO
AND WILTED ONION

‖‖

   4 tablespoons unsalted butter
   2 tablespoons olive oil
  24 snails, soaked in warm water, then rinsed and
     removed from shell (or good-quality canned
     French snails)
   1 tablespoon finely chopped garlic
1 ½ cups thinly sliced onions
     Freshly ground black pepper to taste
   2 ounces prosciutto, cut in narrow 1 ½-inch
     julienne strips
  ½ tablespoon finely chopped fresh parsley
  ½ tablespoon finely chopped chives
   6 slices dark bread (pumpernickel), crust removed,
     toasted

1. Heat butter and oil in a large sauté pan over medium high heat until very hot. Add snails and sauté for 1 minute. Add garlic and toss. Add onions and sauté for about 3 minutes, until soft and transparent. Season with pepper. Add prosciutto and herbs and toss well.

2. Place a slice of toast on each of four warm serving dishes, and divide mixture evenly among the four, allowing six snails per person.

SERVES 4

CHARCUTERIE

RILLETTES

||||||||||||||||||||||||||||||||||||||||||||||||||||||||||||||||||||||||||||||||||||||||||||||||||||||||||||||||||||||||||||||||||||||||||

2½ pounds boneless pork butt, cut into 2-inch
    chunks
¼ cup vegetable oil
1 quart unsalted chicken stock
1 cup dry white wine
1 tablespoon finely chopped garlic
1 teaspoon freshly ground black pepper
7 imported bay leaves
5 whole cloves
    Pinch of dried thyme
    Salt to taste

1. Lightly brown pork chunks in oil in a large heavy saucepan over medium high heat.

2. Add remaining ingredients except salt, and bring to a boil. Reduce heat to medium low. Partially cover and simmer for approximately 1½ hours, until meat is very tender and about 1½ cups liquid remain.

3. Let cool to room temperature, then refrigerate overnight. Discard bay leaves.

4. Using the paddle of an electric mixer or the metal blade of a food processor, combine the meat and fat until the mixture resembles a spread. Be careful not to overbeat. Season with salt and additional black pepper, if desired.

7. Pack rillettes into a crock and serve with crusty French bread, or accompany with a salad for a light meal.

4 CUPS

HEADCHEESE VINAIGRETTE

nexpensive cuts of pork were always poor people's soul food in pig-farming countries. Even the ancient Romans had their equivalent of *charcutiers,* who made all sorts of sausages and other pork products. By the Middle Ages, many countries had developed their own specialties. Our sweetbread-centered *tête de fromage* is a new variation on an old theme. The vinaigrette should be thick, almost like a chopped crudité topping, a refreshing foil to the rich textures of the headcheese.

5 *large pig's knuckles (about 5 pounds total)*
2 *quarts unsalted chicken stock*
1 *quart dry white wine*
1 *large onion, halved crosswise*
1 *large carrot*
1 *spice bag: 12 sprigs of parsley, 5 imported bay leaves, 10 cracked black peppercorns, 8 whole cloves, and a pinch of dried thyme wrapped in a double thickness of cheesecloth and tied with butcher's twine*
  Salt and freshly ground black pepper to taste
2 *large sweetbreads (about ¾ pounds total), rinsed thoroughly and membrane removed*

VINAIGRETTE

¾ *cup olive oil*
¼ *cup red wine vinegar*
¼ *cup diced cucumber*
¼ *cup diced red pepper*
¼ *cup diced yellow or green pepper*
¼ *cup diced onion*
  Salt and freshly ground pepper to taste

1. Combine all headcheese ingredients except salt, pepper, and sweetbreads in a stockpot and bring to a boil over high heat. Skim the surface to remove scum. Reduce heat to medium low and simmer, covered, for 4 hours. Remove the pig's knuckles and let cool.

2. Pour the poaching liquid through a strainer into a bowl and let cool. Discard the vegetables and spice bag. When the pig's knuckles are cool enough to handle, remove bones and discard. Coarsely chop meat and tender gelatinous skin into ½-inch chunks. (There will be about 5 cups.)

3. Poach sweetbreads in boiling salted water to cover, for 10 minutes. Drain. Cool by rinsing under cold running water. Neatly trim and halve lengthwise; then reserve.

4. Combine meat and skin with 3 cups of the strained stock. Taste and season with additional salt and pepper. Pour half of the mixture into a 2-quart loaf pan. Tap the mold against a work surface to settle contents. Place sweetbreads along center of pan, cut side down. Carefully pour in enough remaining meat and stock to fill the pan completely, adding additional stock if needed. Tap mold on a counter and smooth the surface. Cover with plastic wrap and refrigerate overnight, until set.

5. Combine all vinaigrette ingredients in a large mixing bowl and mix thoroughly. Season with salt and pepper.

6. To serve. briefly dip the loaf pan in warm water to loosen, then invert. Carefully cut into ½-inch-thick slices and serve accompanied by vinaigrette dressing.

1 2 ½-INCH SLICES

CHEF ANDRÉ'S WALNUT PÂTÉ

||||||||||||||||||||||||||||||||||||||||||||||||||||||||||||||||||||||||||||||||||||||||||||||||||||||||||||||||||||

2¼ *pounds boneless pork butt, cut into 1-inch chunks*
¾ *pound pork fatback (rind removed), cut into 1-inch pieces*
½ *pound pork liver (skin removed), cut into 1-inch pieces*
1½ *cups chopped onions*
 1 *tablespoon finely chopped shallots*
1½ *cups coarsely broken walnuts*
½ *cup brandy or Cognac*
 1 *tablespoon freshly ground black pepper*
¾ *tablespoon salt*
 5 *imported bay leaves*

1. Coarsely grind pork butt and fatback in a food processor or meat grinder. Finely grind pork liver, onions, and shallots.

2. Combine both mixtures. Add 1 cup of the walnuts, brandy, pepper, and salt. Mix thoroughly; taste and adjust seasoning. Cover mixture and refrigerate overnight.

3. Preheat the oven to 425°F.

4. Pack pâté mixture into a 2-quart pâté mold, preferably oven-proof ceramic. Sprinkle with the remaining ½ cup walnuts, and spread with bay leaves; press walnuts and bay leaves gently into the pâté.

5. Tightly cover the pâté with aluminum foil. Put in a roasting pan and add enough hot water to come three-fourths of the way up the sides of the mold. Bake 1½ hours. Remove the foil and bake an additional half hour, until the pâté is dark and crusty. Let cool to room temperature on a wire rack.

6. Serve in ½-inch-thick slices with stone-ground mustard and cornichons.

SERVES 20

Soups

CHILLED BISQUE OF BROCCOLI AND TURNIP

||||||||||||||||||||||||||||||||||||||||||||||||||||||||||||||||||||||||||||||||||||||||||||||||||||||||||||||||||||||||||||||||

L ouis XIV was so suspicious of his cooks that he would not touch any food until official tasters had tried it. As a result, the soups were lukewarm when they reached him. One day someone chilled the king's soup, and the era of cold soups was born.

¾ cup chopped onion

4 tablespoons unsalted butter

1 large potato, peeled and coarsely chopped

¾ pound turnips, peeled and coarsely chopped

2 bay leaves

  Pinch of dried thyme

1 pound broccoli, washed and coarsely chopped

1 quart chicken stock

1 pint heavy cream

  Salt and freshly ground white pepper to taste

1. In a large saucepan, sauté onion in butter over medium high heat until translucent. Add potato and turnips, and season with bay leaves and thyme. Cook for approximately 8 to 10 minutes. Add broccoli and cook another 3 minutes. Pour in chicken stock and bring to a rolling boil. Partially cover; simmer for one hour.

2. Pour the mixture into a food processor and purée until smooth.

3. In a large saucepan, bring cream to a boil and reduce for 5 to 8 minutes over medium high heat. Add the purée and bring to a rolling boil. Season with salt and pepper. Let soup cool to room temperature. Refrigerate at least 3 to 5 hours before serving.

SERVES 8 TO 10

SEAFOOD GAZPACHO, SIXTY-SEVENTH STREET STYLE

This "drinkable food," as the ancient Greeks called it, has many variations, some made with almonds, mixed with mayonnaise, or, as in our version, flavored with seafood.

2½ pounds red ripe tomatoes, peeled, seeded, and chopped
1 cup coarsely chopped Bermuda onion
½ cup each chopped green pepper and chopped carrot
1 clove of garlic, peeled
5 cups tomato juice
⅓ cup red wine vinegar
Salt and freshly ground black pepper to taste
2 tablespoons olive oil
8 ounces tiny shrimp, shells removed, deveined and lightly cooked
Dash of Louisiana-type hot sauce

GARNISH:
¼ cup chopped fresh dill
6 medium scallions, white part only, washed and cut into ¼-inch dice
1 large cucumber, peeled, seeded, and cut into ¼-inch dice
1 cup freshly toasted croutons

1. Process tomatoes, onion, green pepper, carrot, and garlic in a food processor until the mixture takes on a rough texture.

2. Stir in tomato juice and vinegar, and season with salt and pepper. Whisk in olive oil. Chill for at least 3 hours.

3. Add shrimp. Adjust seasoning with hot sauce, and serve sprinkled with dill in chilled bowls, with crocks of scallion, cucumber, and croutons on the side.

SERVES 8 TO 10

PASTA

FETTUCCINE WITH SAUSAGE, BACON, AND EGGPLANT

5 slices of bacon, cut into ¼-inch pieces

2 tablespoons good-quality Italian olive oil

1 small unpeeled eggplant (about 1 pound), cut into ¼-inch dice, blanched in boiling salted water for 2 minutes, then drained

6 ounces garlic sausage, blanched in boiling water for 3 minutes, drained, skinned, and cut into ¼-inch dice

1½ cups heavy cream

1 pound fettuccine noodles, cooked al dente in rapidly boiling water and drained well
   Salt and freshly ground black pepper to taste

2 tablespoons minced fresh parsley
   Freshly grated Parmesan cheese (Parmigiano Reggiano, if available)

1. In a large skillet, sauté bacon in olive oil until just crisp. Add eggplant and sausage; cook over medium high heat for 3 to 5 minutes, stirring occasionally. Drain off any fat. Add cream and cook until thickened, 3 to 5 minutes.

2. Add pasta and salt and pepper. Toss thoroughly. Transfer to a serving dish and sprinkle with parsley. Serve Parmesan cheese on the side.

SERVES 4

CURRIED SEAFOOD TAGLIATELLE

||||||||||||||||||||||||||||||||||||||||||||||||||||||||||||||||||||||||||||||||||||||||||||||||||||||||||||||||||||

M y wife and I tasted a piquant curried seafood pasta in Sicily. In the course of trying to re-create the exotic combination of flavors in the green-gold-colored sauce, a new dish, only a cousin of its inspiration, emerged.

1 1/2 cups coarsely chopped onions

1/2 cup coarsely chopped carrots

1/2 cup coarsely chopped celery

1 tablespoon finely chopped garlic

1/4 cup clarified unsalted butter

1 1/2 cups diced unpeeled green apple

3/4 cup peeled, seeded, and coarsely chopped tomato

1/2 teaspoon dried thyme

1 bay leaf

1/2 cup dried white wine

1/4 cup tomato purée

1/4 cup high-quality curry powder

1/4 cup all-purpose flour

2 cups unsalted chicken stock, heated to boiling

1/4 cup heavy cream

1/3 cup unsalted butter

1/2 pound medium-size shrimp, peeled, deveined, and cut in half lengthwise

1/2 pound bay scallops

8 ounces fresh mushrooms, thinly sliced

1 pound dried tagliatelle (thin fettuccine noodles), cooked al dente, drained, tossed with 1 tablespoon vegetable oil, and kept warm

2 tablespoons minced fresh parsley

1. In a large heavy saucepan, sauté onion, carrot, celery, and garlic in clarified butter over medium low heat about 6 minutes, until vegetables are softened.

2. Add apple, tomato, thyme, and bay leaf. Continue cooking 5 minutes, stirring occasionally.

3. Add wine and tomato purée. Cook, stirring often, until almost all the liquid has evaporated, about 5 minutes.

4. Stir in curry powder and flour. Stir and cook for 3 minutes.

5. Gradually add chicken stock, stirring constantly. Reduce heat to low and simmer, uncovered, 15 to 20 minutes, stirring to make sure the sauce doesn't stick to the bottom of the pan.

6. Add cream and simmer 5 minutes.

7. Strain the sauce through a sieve, pressing the vegetables with the back of a spoon. Keep the sauce warm.

8. Melt the butter in a very large skillet over medium heat.

9. Add shrimp, scallops, and mushrooms; sauté until shrimp just turn pink.

10. Add cooked pasta and curry sauce and toss until thoroughly combined.

11. Transfer to a serving plate. Sprinkle with parsley and serve immediately.

SERVES 8 AS APPETIZER OR 4 AS MAIN COURSE

GNOCCHI PARISIENNE

Virtually all European dumplings, including noques, nockerl, knödel, knedliky, and nokkedli, are derived from the Italian gnocchi. This light French version seems almost souffléed.

GNOCCHI PASTE

   1 cup plus 1½ tablespoons all-purpose flour
  ¾ cup freshly grated Parmesan cheese
    Pinch of freshly grated nutmeg
    Pinch of salt and freshly ground white pepper to taste
   1 cup plus 2 tablespoons milk
   5 tablespoons unsalted butter, cut into pieces
   3 eggs

SAUCE

  ½ cup heavy cream
   4 tablespoons unsalted butter, cut into pieces
    Pinch of freshly grated nutmeg
    Pinch of freshly ground white pepper
   1 cup freshly grated Parmesan cheese
   1 tablespoon melted unsalted butter

1. To make the gnocchi paste combine flour, ¾ cup Parmesan cheese, nutmeg, and salt and pepper.

2. Bring milk and 5 tablespoons butter to a boil in a large saucepan over high heat, then immediately reduce the heat to medium high. Add the flour mixture and stir constantly with a wooden spoon until a smooth paste that pulls away from the sides of the pan is formed. Remove from heat and let rest 3 minutes, stirring several times.

3. Using a wooden spoon or electric mixer, vigorously beat in the eggs, one at a time, until thoroughly incorporated. (Do not over-work the mixture.) Let cool slightly.

4. Line two large baking sheets with wax paper and sprinkle with flour.

5. Spoon the paste into a pastry bag fitted with a ½-inch plain tip. Squeeze out 1¼-inch lengths of paste onto the wax paper. Neatly cut off lengths of paste using a knife dipped in cold water.

6. Sprinkle gnocchi with flour. Cover and chill for 30 minutes, or up to several hours.

7. Bring 5 quarts of lightly salted water to a boil in a very large pot. Quickly add gnocchi to water, one at a time, using a rubber spatula to lift them off the wax paper.

8. When the water returns to a boil, reduce heat to medium low and let simmer. Remove gnocchi with a slotted spoon as they rise to the surface; drain well, and put in a baking dish large enough to hold them in one layer.

9. Preheat the broiler.

10. To make the sauce, put cream, 4 tablespoons butter, nutmeg, and pepper in a small saucepan and bring to a boil over high heat. Stir in half the Parmesan cheese and cook for 2 to 3 minutes over medium high heat.

11. Pour sauce over gnocchi. Sprinkle the remaining Parmesan cheese over the gnocchi and top with melted butter. Broil until golden brown and bubbling. Serve hot.

SERVES 4 AS MAIN COURSE

PASTA WITH SPINACH PESTO

||||||||||||||||||||||||||||||||||||||||||||||||||||||||||||||||||||||||||||||||||||||||||||||||||||||||||||||||||||||||||||||||||||||||||

This variation on the traditional sauce is a great comfort to pesto-lovers when basil is not available. If serving pasta without Parmesan cheese, increase the amount of salt accordingly.

> 2 *pounds fresh spinach, washed well, stems and large veins removed*
> 1 *tablespoon finely chopped garlic*
> 1 *cup olive oil*
> ½ *cup pine nuts*
> 1½ *pounds fresh fettuccine or 1 pound dried, cooked* al dente *in boiling salted water and drained*
> *Salt and white pepper to taste, preferably freshly ground*
> *Freshly grated Parmesan cheese to taste*

1. Place spinach and 1 cup of water in a large saucepan. Cover and cook over medium high heat until spinach is wilted; it should take just a couple of minutes. Drain spinach in a colander, squeezing out as much liquid as possible. Finely chop spinach in a food processor or by hand. Combine with garlic.

2. Heat oil in a large skillet over medium high heat until very hot. Add pine nuts and sauté until lightly golden, about 2 to 3 minutes. Reduce heat to low, add spinach mixture to pan, and cook 3 minutes.

3. Toss in cooked pasta, cooking just until heated through, and season to taste with salt and pepper.

4. Divide pasta among four heated bowls and serve accompanied by Parmesan cheese.

SERVES 4

SEAFOOD STEWS

BOURRIDE WITH AÏOLI

|||||||||||||||||||||||||||||||||||||||||||||||||||||||||||||||||||||||||||||||||||||||||||||||||||||||||||||||||||||||||||||||||||||||||

B ourride is a second cousin of bouillabaisse, a soup-stew enriched by two important staples of Provence: very fresh garlic and local olive oil. Our version is based on bourrides I've known in and around the homes and restaurants of Marseilles.

FISH STOCK

1 1/2 cups thinly sliced onions

 1/2 cup thinly sliced celery

   1 cup thinly sliced leek, white part only

 1/4 cup olive oil

   3 cloves of garlic, peeled

   3 pounds fish bones from scrod, sea bass, or other
      nonoily fish

 12 sprigs of parsley

   1 bay leaf

 1/2 tablespoon fennel seeds

   1 teaspoon dried thyme

 1/2 teaspoon coriander seeds

   2 tablespoons unsalted butter

   2 tablespoons all-purpose flour
      Salt and freshly ground white pepper to taste

AÏOLI

5 large cloves of garlic, peeled
⅛ teaspoon saffron threads
3 egg yolks
1 cup olive oil
1 tablespoon plus 1 teaspoon fresh lemon juice
  Salt and freshly ground black pepper to taste

SEAFOOD

  10-ounce sea bass fillet, cut crosswise into
  quarters
  8-ounce scrod fillet, cut crosswise into quarters
  8-ounce piece of monkfish, cut crosswise into
  quarters
12 large mussels, scrubbed and beards removed
 4 3½-inch strips of orange rind (orange part
  only), removed with a vegetable peeler

1. To prepare fish stock, sauté onion, celery, and leek in ¼ cup oil in a large pot over medium heat for about 6 minutes until soft and translucent. Do not allow to brown. Add garlic and continue to cook for 5 minutes, stirring. Add fish bones and 1 quart cold water. Bring to a boil over high heat. Add parsley, bay leaf, fennel, thyme, and coriander; reduce heat to low and simmer, covered, for 2 hours.

2. Melt butter in a small saucepan over low heat. Whisk in flour; stir and cook 3 to 5 minutes. Do not allow to color; remove from heat.

3. After the stock has simmered for 1 hour and 40 minutes, remove 1 cup and, whisking constantly, gradually pour it into the roux (butter-flour mixture), stirring over low heat until the mixture is smooth and thickened. Bring to a boil. Whisk into the pot and continue cooking for 20 minutes.

4. Prepare aïoli by crushing garlic using a mortar and pestle. Add saffron and pound until garlic begins to color. Remove to a medium-size bowl.

5. Whisk egg yolks into garlic mixture. Then whisk in the oil, in a slow steady stream, until the mixture resembles a very thick mayonnaise. (Be careful not to add oil too quickly, as this can make the mixture separate.) Whisk in lemon juice and season with salt and black pepper.

6. Pour fish stock through a strainer into a large bowl. Discard vegetables and fish bones. Season with salt and white pepper. Keep warm.

7. Divide seafood and orange strips among four flameproof casseroles with matching lids. Pour ¾ cup fish stock into each casserole; cover. Cook over medium heat for 5 to 8 minutes, until the thickest pieces of fish are just cooked through. Remove from heat.

8. Pour hot stock from one of the casseroles into a bowl. Quickly whisk in 3 tablespoons aïoli. Pour the aïoli-flavored liquid over the seafood in casserole, cover, and keep warm. Repeat with the three remaining portions.

9. Serve bourride in the individual casseroles set on heatproof plates. Serve remaining aïoli on the side.

SERVES 4 AS MAIN COURSE

MOULES HONFLEUR

Cleaning the mussels thoroughly is essential for any recipe, unless you like sand in your seafood. Honfleur is the quaint little port in Normandy, and mussels are served in this manner in several of its restaurants. This dish was part of the Four Seasons' menu in the mid-1960s.

56 large mussels, scrubbed well and beards removed
1½ cups dry white wine
 1 cup heavy cream
 4 tablespoons unsalted butter, cut into pieces
 1 tablespoon plus 1 teaspoon chopped shallots
 1 tablespoon plus 1 teaspoon chopped fresh
    parsley
 2 teaspoons freshly ground white pepper

1. Combine all ingredients in a large saucepan. Cook, covered, over medium high heat, stirring once or twice, until mussels just begin to open, about 3 to 5 minutes. With a slotted spoon remove mussels to a large bowl; cover and keep warm.

2. Cook mussel liquid over high heat for 10 minutes. Divide mussels and liquid among four heated shallow soup plates and serve.

SERVES 4 AS MAIN COURSE

FISH & SHELLFISH

CALIFORNIA LAKE STURGEON, MILANESE STYLE

||||||||||||||||||||||||||||||||||||||||||||||||||||||||||||||||||||||||||||||||||||||||||||||||||||||||||||||||||||||||||||||

W ho knows why sturgeon is served almost exclusively smoked, when, cooked in its fresh state, the texture and pale white color of this fish recall a cutlet of especially young veal.

8 thin slices of lake sturgeon (about 3 ounces each)
  Salt and freshly ground black pepper
  All-purpose flour for dredging
3 eggs, lightly beaten
1 1/2 cups freshly made bread crumbs
1/2 cup olive oil or clarified butter
4 tablespoons unsalted butter
2 lemons, cut in half crosswise

1. Season sturgeon slices on both sides with salt and pepper. Dust slices in flour, shaking off excess. Dip into eggs and then coat with bread crumbs, pressing crumbs firmly into sturgeon.

2. Heat oil in a large sauté pan over medium high heat. When it is very hot, add the sturgeon and sauté for 2 minutes on each side. Remove the sturgeon from the pan to paper towels, to absorb excess fat. Keep warm.

3. Drain the fat from the pan. Add butter to the pan and cook over high heat until the butter becomes nut brown in color.

4. Put two slices of sturgeon on each of four warm serving plates, and pour a portion of brown butter over each. Serve at once with lemon on the side.

SERVES 4

BAY SCALLOPS SAUTÉED
WITH SHALLOTS AND WALNUTS

This dish is best when prepared with the light olive oil of Tuscany or southern France, which will not overpower the taste of the delicate scallops.

2 *pounds bay scallops*
6 *tablespoons unsalted butter*
4 *tablespoons olive oil*
4 *teaspoons finely chopped shallots*
¾ *cup toasted walnuts, coarsely broken*
4 *teaspoons finely chopped chives*
    Salt and freshly ground white pepper to taste
4 *lemon wedges*

1. Pat scallops dry with paper towels.

2. Heat butter and oil in a large sauté pan over medium heat, until hot. Add scallops and sauté for 2 to 3 minutes. Add shallots and toss. Add walnuts and chives and cook another minute.

3. Drain off excess fat and season with salt and pepper. Divide onto four warm serving plates. Serve at once with lemon.

SERVES 4

SWORDFISH STEAK TOPPED WITH SOFT-SHELL CRAB

CRABS

    4 *medium-size soft-shell crabs, rinsed*
    All-purpose flour for dredging
    6 *tablespoons unsalted butter*
    Salt and freshly ground black pepper to taste

SWORDFISH

    4 *6-ounce swordfish steaks, approximately 1¼ inches thick*
    2 *tablespoons melted unsalted butter*
    Salt and freshly ground white pepper to taste

GARNISH:

    4 *lemon halves, cut into crown shapes*

1. Pat crabs dry with paper towels. Lightly dredge in flour, shaking off any excess.

2. Heat 6 tablespoons butter in a large sauté pan until hot. Add crabs and sauté gently over medium heat for approximately 5 minutes on each side. Season with salt and pepper.

3. While crabs are cooking, lightly brush the swordfish steaks on both sides with 2 tablespoons melted butter. Season with salt and pepper and broil for approximately 3 minutes on each side under a preheated broiler.

4. When crabs and swordfish are finished, place each swordfish steak on a warm serving dish. Top with a crab, garnish with a lemon half, and serve at once.

SERVES 4

HOT SMOKED SALMON

You can set up the fish before dinner, but light the fire just as you sit down to the first course. Care must be taken not to obliterate the subtle flavor of the salmon by oversmoking.

Birch or oak sawdust, for smoking
4 6-ounce salmon fillets, boned and skinned
1 tablespoon olive oil
Salt and freshly ground black pepper to taste

1. Remove the rack from a small broiler pan. Sprinkle a light dusting of sawdust over the entire bottom of the broiler pan, so that the surface is just covered. Replace the rack.

2. Using a pastry brush, lightly coat both sides of the salmon fillets with olive oil. Season well with salt and pepper.

3. Place the seasoned fillets, skinned side down, on the rack in the broiler pan. Tightly cover the pan with aluminum foil.

4. Put the broiler pan on a burner over medium heat and cook for 8 to 10 minutes. Open one corner of the foil and check for doneness. The salmon should be just flaky when tested with a fork. Serve immediately.

SERVES 4

MEAT & BIRD

POT-AU-FEU

C hildhood comes back to me with the arresting aroma of a pot-au-feu. Escoffier called it the symbol of family life, and Mirabeau, the French eighteenth-century revolutionary hero, went perilously far out on a metaphoric limb to say: "In the common pot-au-feu lies the foundation of the Empire."

6 pounds short ribs of beef
3 pounds beef brisket
1 veal shank (about 3 pounds)
   Coarse salt (kosher salt or sea salt)
1 spice bag: 6 sprigs of parsley, 1 sprig of fresh
   thyme, 2 teaspoons cracked black peppercorns,
   and 1 bay leaf wrapped in a double thickness
   of cheesecloth and tied with butcher's twine
1 onion, peeled and cut in half, each half studded
   with 2 cloves
3 pounds marrowbones, each cut to about 6-inch
   length and pieces individually wrapped in
   cheesecloth with both ends tied
1 3- to 4-pound fowl
10 small carrots, peeled and tied in a bunch
1 medium-size knob of celery, peeled and
   quartered
5 leeks, trimmed, sliced in half lengthwise,
   washed well to remove sand, and tied in a bunch
10 small turnips, peeled and trimmed
   Freshly ground white pepper to taste

TABLE CONDIMENTS

Coarse salt

Cornichons

Dijon mustard

Dark stone-ground mustard

Fresh Creamed Horseradish Sauce (recipe follows)

Toast, for marrow

1. Put ribs, beef brisket, and veal shank in a deep soup pot; add salt and enough cold water to cover the meat (about 6 quarts) and bring to a simmer.

2. Add a few tablespoons of cold water to retard boiling in order to remove foam from the surface. Keep skimming as necessary.

3. Add spice bag and studded onion halves and simmer, uncovered, for about 2 hours.

4. Add marrowbones and fowl and continue to simmer for 1 hour. Skim foam from time to time.

5. Add vegetables and simmer approximately 45 minutes more, removing each vegetable when it becomes tender (test by pricking with a fork).

6. Remove string from cooked vegetables, and keep them warm by putting in a small pot with some of the cooking stock. Do not place over direct heat or vegetables will overcook.

7. Drain cooking stock from meats and keep meats warm (as above with vegetables).

8. Strain stock through moistened cheesecloth into another soup pot. Bring to a simmer. Skim off any fat, and season to taste with coarse salt and white pepper.

9. Discard spice bag and remove cheesecloth from marrowbones.

10. Remove chicken and reserve for another use. (It can be the basis of a particularly flavorful chicken salad.)

CREAMED HORSERADISH SAUCE

 6 tablespoons freshly grated (or drained and rinsed bottled) horseradish
1½ cups heavy cream
 2 teaspoons Dijon mustard
 2 tablespoons white wine vinegar
 Pinch of salt

1. Combine all ingredients in a mixing bowl and blend well.

2. Adjust seasoning to taste with a bit more mustard or a pinch of salt. Serve at room temperature.

SETTING THE STAGE

1. Put short ribs and veal shank on a heated oval platter with a lip.

2. Garnish by surrounding meats with vegetables. Arrange marrowbones on top.

3. Moisten entire platter with some of the simmering bouillon. Cover bouillon and keep hot.

SERVICE

1. Serve bouillon in cups as a first course.

2. Pass thinly sliced hot toast and marrowbones along with individual marrow spoons. Coarse salt should be on the table.

3. Sliced brisket of beef and the short ribs are served with the vegetables as a separate course. Sauce and condiments are offered as an accompaniment.

SERVES 10

LAMB AND DUCK
CASSOULET WITH LENTILS

||||||||||||||||||||||||||||||||||||||||||||||||||||||||||||||||||||||||||||||||||||||||||||||||||||||||||||||||||||||||||||||

Cassoulet is an immigrant from the Middle East, where origi-
nally it was made with chickpeas, lamb, and olive oil. When
the Jews left Palestine in the Middle Ages, they brought this dish,
served for the traditional Sabbath meal, with them to France. Its
French name comes from *cassolo,* the earthenware casserole made
in the town of Issel, near Castelnaudary. To simplify this recipe,
we eliminated instructions on making *confit* of goose or duck,
traditionally part of cassoulet, which we feel won't be missed.

> 1 *pound lentils, soaked in cold water for an hour*
>   *and drained*
> 1 *ounce olive oil*
> 1 *pound boneless lamb, cut in medium-size pieces*
> 12 *ounces boneless duck meat (leg and thigh meat*
>   *is best), cut into medium-size pieces*
>   *Freshly ground black pepper*
> 1 *pound bacon, cut into 1-inch pieces*
> 1 1/2 *tablespoons finely chopped garlic*
> 2 *red ripe tomatoes, peeled, seeded, and coarsely*
>   *chopped*
> 1/2 *cup tomato purée*
> 1 *onion, peeled and cut in half crosswise*
> 4 *bay leaves*
> 6 *cloves*
>   *Pinch of thyme*
> 2 *quarts rich beef stock*
> 12 *ounces garlic sausage, blanched and cut into*
>   *1/2-inch dice*
>   *Salt to taste*
> 1 *cup bread crumbs*
> 4 *tablespoons chopped fresh parsley*
> 4 *tablespoons butter, melted*

1. Put lentils in a large saucepan and cover with plenty of cold water.

2. Bring to a quick boil and cook over medium high heat for 10 to 12 minutes, or until tender. Drain.

3. Heat oil in a large saucepan and when very hot add the lamb.

4. Sear the lamb evenly on all sides, cooking for about 3 minutes.

5. Add the duck and continue to cook for another 3 to 5 minutes.

6. Season meats well with pepper. Add bacon to pan and stir well, then add garlic and cook for 5 minutes more. Stir in chopped tomatoes and tomato purée.

7. Stud the onion halves by attaching two bay leaves with three cloves to each. Add to saucepan; season with thyme, add stock, and bring to a boil.

8. Reduce heat, cover, and cook over medium heat for 1¼ hours, skimming off scum from time to time. Remove cover, stir in cooked lentils, and continue slowly cooking the mixture, uncovered, for another 30 minutes. Remove studded onion halves and discard.

9. Add sausage and cook an additional 10 minutes. Season with salt and papper.

10. In a small bowl, toss together bread crumbs and parsley.

11. To serve, ladle each portion of cassoulet into a shallow ovenproof earthenware dish, approximately 1½ inches deep, and lightly coat with bread crumbs.

12. Brush surface with a small amount of butter, and place under a preheated broiler for 3 minutes, or until golden brown. Serve at once.

SERVES 10

ııı

  4 cups crustless day-old French bread, cut into
     ½-inch cubes

 ¾ cup milk

12 ounces fresh chestnuts, cooked in boiling water
     for about 15 minutes, then peeled and skinned
     (or 1 pound can water-packed chestnuts)

  1 cup chopped onion

  1 tablespoon chopped shallot

  1 teaspoon chopped garlic

  7 tablespoons unsalted butter

  6 ounces of veal, cut into 1-inch chunks

  6 ounces of pork, cut into 1-inch chunks

 ¼ cup heavy cream

  1 egg, lightly beaten

  2 tablespoons brandy (optional)

  3 bay leaves

  1 teaspoon dried thyme
     Salt and freshly ground black pepper to taste

  1 5-pound veal breast, boned and pocketed
     (reserve bones)
     Vegetable oil

1½ cups chopped onions

  1 cup chopped celery

  1 cup chopped carrots

  1 cup dry white wine

1½ cups unsalted beef stock

1. Preheat the oven to 425°F.

2. Combine bread and milk in a bowl and let soak until milk is absorbed. Squeeze out excess milk and discard.

3. Coarsely chop half the chestnuts.

4. Sauté 1 cup chopped onion, shallot, and garlic in 3 tablespoons butter in a medium skillet until soft. Add chopped chestnuts and cook for 2 to 3 minutes longer. Let cool.

5. In a bowl blend the veal, pork, bread, and sautéed onion mixture. Force the mixture through the medium disk of a food grinder, or grind in a food processor by using an on and off pulsing action.

6. Thoroughly combine the ground mixture with the remaining chestnuts, cream, egg, brandy, bay leaves, thyme, and salt and pepper. Stuff the mixture into veal breast pocket. Using butcher's twine, sew up pocket opening to enclose stuffing.

7. Put reserved veal bones in a lightly oiled roasting pan. Brush the veal breast with oil on all sides; set on top of bones. Cover with aluminum foil. Roast the veal for 1½ hours, basting several times with pan juices.

8. Remove foil and add onion, celery, and carrot to pan. Reduce the temperature to 375°F and continue roasting 45 minutes longer, until veal is golden brown. Remove veal from pan and keep warm.

9. Add wine to pan and deglaze by scraping up browned bits with a wooden spoon over medium heat. Strain pan liquid into a medium saucepan.

10. Discard vegetables and add beef stock and cook over high heat until reduced to about 1 cup, about 10 minutes. Season with salt and pepper. Remove from heat and whisk in the remaining 4 tablespoons butter.

11. To serve, remove twine and cut veal into 1-inch-thick slices. Lightly coat with sauce and serve.

SERVES 6

BLANQUETTE OF VEAL, SWEETBREADS, AND CHICKEN

|||||||||||||||||||||||||||||||||||||||||||||||||||||||||||||||||||||||||||||||||||||||||||||||||||||||||||||||||||||||||||||||||||||||||

Although the term *blanquette* refers to a thick sauce that blankets meat and vegetables, our version produces a much lighter dish than the standard preparations.

   3 *pounds veal, cut into 1½-inch chunks*
   2 *quarts unsalted chicken stock*
1½ *cups chopped onions*
   1 *cup chopped carrots*
   1 *cup chopped celery*
   1 *spice bag: 6 sprigs of parsley, 3 bay leaves, 10 cracked black peppercorns, 6 whole cloves, and ½ teaspoon dried thyme wrapped in a double thickness of cheesecloth and tied with butcher's twine*
   1 *pound sweetbreads, rinsed thoroughly and membrane removed*
  ½ *pound boneless and skinless chicken breast*
  ⅔ *cup unsalted butter*
   1 *cup all-purpose flour*
   1 *quart heavy cream*
     Salt and freshly ground white pepper to taste
   4 *tablespoons unsalted butter, at room temperature*
  24 *quarter-size mushrooms, stems removed*
     Juice of 2 lemons
  24 *small white onions (no larger than walnut-size), peeled*
     Rice pilaf

1. Put veal, chicken stock, onion, carrot, celery, and spice bag in a large saucepan and bring to a boil over high heat. Skim the surface to remove scum.

2. Reduce heat to medium low and simmer slowly for about 40 minutes, until veal is tender.

3. Add sweetbreads and chicken to saucepan. Continue cooking for 10 minutes.

4. Pour veal mixture through a strainer over a large bowl. Reserve strained stock and meats. Discard vegetables and spice bag. Cut sweetbreads into ¼-inch-thick slices and chicken into ¼-inch-thick strips. Set aside with cooked veal.

5. Melt ⅔ cup butter in a large saucepan. Whisk in flour. Cook, stirring, over medium low heat for 2 to 3 minutes. Do not allow to darken.

6. Gradually whisk in 1 quart of the strained stock to make a smooth sauce. Bring to a boil, then reduce heat to medium low and simmer for 45 minutes, stirring occasionally. Whisk in cream. Increase heat to medium and cook for 10 minutes. Thin the sauce by adding ½ cup more reserved stock. Taste and season with salt and pepper. Remove pan from heat and whisk in 4 tablespoons butter to finish the sauce.

7. Cook mushrooms in lemon juice and enough water to cover in a small saucepot over medium heat until tender, about 5 minutes. Remove with a slotted spoon to a bowl.

8. In the same pot, cook onions until tender, about 10 minutes. Remove with a slotted spoon to the bowl with the mushrooms.

9. To serve, add veal, sweetbreads, chicken, mushrooms, and onions to sauce. Reheat thoroughly. Serve blanquette with rice pilaf.

SERVES 10

TRIPE AUX PRUNEAUX

There is a secret brotherhood of tripe lovers, and they are just as misunderstood as the Rosicrucians were in the Middle Ages. This particular version is based on uncooked beef tripe, though ethnic Italian, French, and Portuguese butchers often sell it already cooked. Tripe, a texture food, is a perfect carrier of taste. The surprising combination in this recipe yields a sinewy, silky fusion of flavors and lip-smacking texture.

10 pounds calves' feet

6 pounds honeycomb tripe, cut into 1 1/2-inch
    triangles

2 1/4 gallons unsalted beef stock

1 quart dry white wine

6 large carrots, peeled

2 large onions, peeled

1/4 cup tomato purée

1 spice bag: 10 bay leaves, 8 black peppercorns,
    6 parsley sprigs, 6 whole cloves, 1 bulb of
    garlic, halved, and 1 tablespoon dried thyme
    wrapped in a double thickness of cheesecloth
    and tied with butcher's twine

1 cup chopped carrots

1 pound pitted prunes

1/4 cup Calvados or applejack
    Salt and freshly ground black pepper to taste

10 medium-size boiled potatoes, peeled

1. In two separate bowls, soak calves' feet and tripe in water to cover overnight in the refrigerator. Drain.

2. Preheat the oven to 350°F.

3. In two separate large saucepans, blanch calves' feet and tripe in boiling salted water for 15 minutes. Drain.

4. Combine calves' feet, stock, wine, whole carrots, onions, tomato purée, and spice bag in a very large stockpot and bring to a rolling boil on top of the stove.

5. Remove from heat, cover with a tight-fitting lid, and put in the oven. Let simmer for 5 hours.

6. Remove calves' feet. Add tripe to stockpot and return to oven to cook for 2 hours.

7. Remove carrots, onions, and spice bag; discard. Add chopped carrots to pot and continue cooking for an additional 30 minutes.

8. When calves' feet are cool enough to handle, remove bones and discard. Chop tender skin and usable meat into ½-inch chunks.

9. Transfer stockpot to stove top. Using a strainer, remove tripe and chopped carrots to a bowl; keep warm. Cook stock over high heat until reduced to 8 cups, about 30 minutes. Reduce heat to medium. Add meats, chopped carrots, prunes, and Calvados to pot. Cook 10 minutes. Taste and season with salt and pepper.

10. To serve, pour over potatoes in shallow soup bowls.

SERVES 10

CHEF ANDRÉ'S GARLIC CHICKEN

IIIIIIIIIIIIIIIIIIIIIIIIIIIIIIIIIIIIIIIIIIIIIIIIIIIIIIIIIIIIIIIIIIIIIIIIIIIIIIIIIIIIIIIIIIIIIIIIIIIIIIIIIIIIIIIIIIIIIII

During the six-month restoration of the Café in 1975, chef André Guillou, director Steve Gurgely, and I tasted hundreds of recipes. One day, trying to indicate the style of its future cuisine, I said to André: "Why don't you cook something your mother made when you were growing up in Britanny?" The recipe that follows is the first written version of this ancestral dish.

  2 2½-pound chickens
     Salt and freshly ground black pepper to taste
  ¼ cup olive oil
 20 cloves of garlic, thinly sliced
  6 imported bay leaves
 1½ cups coarsely chopped onions
  ¾ cup coarsely chopped carrots
  ¾ cup coarsely chopped celery
  1 cup dry white wine
  1 quart unsalted chicken stock
 10 shallots, thinly sliced
  4 tablespoons unsalted butter, softened

1. Preheat oven to 375°F.

2. Season chickens inside and out with salt and pepper. Gently separate skin from breast meat, breaking the center membrane that attaches skin to meat.

3. Holding the skin away from the breast, spread 1 tablespoon olive oil over the breast meat of each chicken. Evenly distribute half the sliced garlic and the 6 bay leaves over the breast meat.

4. Toss onion, carrot, and celery in a bowl. Stuff chicken cavities with as much of the vegetables as they can hold. Reserve remaining vegetables. Sew chickens closed with butcher's twine.

5. Brush chickens with the remaining olive oil. Put them in a roasting pan; roast for 30 minutes, basting from time to time.

6. Reduce the temperature to 350°F. Add reserved vegetables to pan and continue to roast until juices run clear when chicken is pierced, about 30 minutes more, basting chickens from time to time with pan juices. Remove chickens from pan and keep warm.

7. Sauté pan vegetables in the roasting pan over medium heat until caramel-colored, about 3 to 5 minutes. Do not let them burn. Add wine to pan and deglaze by scraping up browned bits with a wooden spoon. Cook over high heat until reduced to ½ cup, about 4 to 6 minutes. Add chicken stock; reduce heat and simmer, uncovered, for 15 minutes. Strain sauce through a fine sieve into a medium saucepan, forcing as much of the vegetables through as possible.

8. Meanwhile, blanch the remaining sliced garlic and the shallots for 3 minutes in 1½ cups boiling water in a medium saucepan. Drain and add to strained sauce. Reduce sauce over high heat until thick enough to coat the back of a spoon, about 15 to 20 minutes. Remove saucepan from heat. Taste and season with salt and pepper, if needed. Whisk in butter, a tablespoon at a time. Keep the sauce warm.

9. Using poultry shears or a large heavy knife, split chickens in half by cutting first through breastbone and then through backbone. Discard butcher's twine. Remove vegetable stuffing and discard. Cut each chicken half into four serving pieces.

10. To serve, arrange chicken on heated serving plates, lightly coat with some sauce, and serve. Serve remaining sauce on the side.

SERVES 4

ROULADE OF BEEF, AUSTRIAN HOUSEWIFE STYLE

||||||||||||||||||||||||||||||||||||||||||||||||||||||||||||||||||||||||||||||||||||||||||||||||||||||||||||||||||||||||||||||||||||

Executive Chef Thomas Ferlesch, who was born in Vienna, remembers this typical Austrian and German dish from his childhood. Nowadays, it has migrated from home kitchens to well-known European restaurants, where it is called *Rindsroulade Nach Hausfrauen Art*. It fits comfortably on the Café's *bourgeoise* menu, where we serve it with kohlrabi, carrots, new potatoes or—in the winter—*spätzle*.

    2 medium onions, cut into quarters
    3 tablespoons vegetable oil
    4 paillards of beef, about 11 ounces each [these
       can be made from top or bottom round; ask
       your butcher to pound the meat as thinly as
       possible]
    2 tablespoons Dijon mustard
    1 teaspoon salt
    ¾ teaspoon freshly ground black pepper
    1 large Kosher dill pickle, cut lengthwise into
       thin slices
    4 slices bacon
    ¼ cup all-purpose flour
    2 cups chicken or beef stock
    1 cup sour cream
    1 cup dry red wine
 1½ tablespoons tomato paste
    2 tablespoons Hungarian paprika

1. Sauté the onions in one tablespoon of the oil just until translucent, about 5 minutes. Remove the onions with a slotted spoon.

2. Lay out all four paillards on a large surface. Season each with ½ tablespoon mustard, salt, and pepper. Scatter equal amounts of sautéed onion evenly over each paillard, then lay equal amounts of dill pickle slices lengthwise over each. Lay one bacon slice over each paillard. Roll up paillards tightly and tie each one with kitchen twine in three places so the roulades will stay closed.

3. Place the flour in a large plate and roll the roulades in the flour until completely covered on all surfaces. Pat off excess flour.

4. Preheat the oven to 375°F.

5. Heat the remaining oil in a heavy ovenproof medium-size frying pan over high heat. Sear prepared roulades until they are brown on all sides. Discard excess fat. Pour 2 cups water into the pan and reduce the heat to medium-high; cook, uncovered, for 5 minutes, scraping the bottom of the pan a few times to release the browned bits of meat. Add the chicken or beef stock, sour cream, red wine, tomato paste, and paprika.

6. Put the pan, uncovered, into the oven for 45 minutes. Remove the roulades from the sauce, cut off the string, and keep warm while you finish the sauce.

7. Strain the sauce, if you like a smoother consistency, and put into a saucepan over medium-high heat. Simmer until the sauce is reduced and lightly thickened (it should coat the back of a spoon). Taste for seasoning; you may want to add salt, pepper, and/or a bit of sugar.

8. Serve at once. Or refrigerate the roulades and sauce together to serve in one or two days, when you should cover and reheat slowly, over low heat on top of the stove or in a 300°F. oven, until meat is heated through.

SERVES 4

CALF'S LIVER WITH SESAME AND MUSTARD CRUST

○○

However circuitous the route, one often returns to the beginning, and the pungent crust of this dish is just a recollection of my mother's breaded calf's liver.

8 2-ounce slices of calf's liver
   Freshly ground black pepper to taste
1 cup sesame seeds
1 cup yellow mustard seeds
3 tablespoons Dijon mustard
4 tablespoons unsalted butter
4 tablespoons olive oil

1. Season liver slices with pepper.

2. In a shallow plate, combine sesame and mustard seeds.

3. Lightly brush each liver slice on both sides with mustard, then dredge on both sides in sesame and mustard seed mixture, pressing seeds firmly into liver to coat.

4. Heat butter and oil in a large sauté pan over medium high heat. When the fat is hot, slip in the liver slices and sauté for 2 minutes on each side. The seeds should be golden brown, but not at all burned.

5. Remove liver from pan and pat off excess fat with paper towels. Serve at once on warm serving plates.

SERVES 4

BRUNCHES

SCRAMBLED EGGS IN BRIOCHE WITH GRAVLAX
||||||||||||||||||||||||||||||||||||||||||||||||||||||||||||||||||||||||||||||||||||||||||||||||||||||||||||||||||||||||||||||||||

12 eggs
   Salt and freshly ground black pepper to taste
 8 tablespoons unsalted butter
16 thin slices gravlax (see page 30)
 4 brioches, split in half and toasted

GARNISH:
 4 sprigs of dill

1. Break eggs into a large mixing bowl and whisk with a fork until well blended. Season with salt and pepper.

2. In a large sauté or frying pan melt butter over medium high heat. When butter is hot, pour in beaten eggs. Using a rubber spatula or wooden spoon, stir and cook eggs until they just begin to set and are no longer runny. Do not overcook or they will dry out.

3. Divide eggs among four warm serving dishes, place toasted brioche alongside, and attractively arrange four slices of gravlax around each plate.

4. Garnish with dill and serve at once.

SERVES 4

SMOKED SALMON BENEDICT, CAFÉ DES ARTISTES

Lemmuel Benedict, a Wall Street stockbroker, used to order toast, a few slices of crisp bacon, two poached eggs, and a gooseneck of hollandaise sauce at the Waldorf Astoria's Men's Bar. Oscar of the Waldorf eventually exchanged the toast for English muffin, the bacon for ham, then added truffle slices and a few drops of *glace de viande,* a concentrated meat extract. I, in turn, made changes to accommodate eggs Benedict addicts of the smoked salmon persuasion.

BÉARNAISE SAUCE

- 2 *tablespoons chopped fresh tarragon leaves*
- 3 *tablespoons tarragon vinegar (white wine vinegar may be substituted)*
- 2 *tablespoons finely chopped shallots*
- 1 *teaspoon freshly ground black pepper*
- 1⅓ *cups dry white wine*
- 6 *egg yolks*
- 2 *cups unsalted butter, diced and at room temperature*

  Salt and cayenne pepper to taste

  Juice of 1 lemon plus more fresh lemon juice to taste

- 8 *eggs*
- 4 *English muffins, split*
- 16 *thin slices smoked salmon (approximately ½ pound)*

GARNISH:

  Fresh watercress or other green herb sprig

1. To make the béarnaise sauce, combine tarragon, vinegar, shallots, pepper, and wine in a large saucepan. Bring to a boil over medium high heat and reduce to ¼ cup of liquid. Remove from heat and let cool.

2. To complete the sauce, combine egg yolks and 2 tablespoons water in the top of a double boiler and whisk until lemony in color. Continue whisking over simmering water until the mixture is light and fluffy. Add pieces of butter, one at a time, whisking until completely incorporated. Strain through a fine sieve into a small bowl. Season with salt, cayenne pepper, and lemon juice to taste. Whisk in cooled tarragon reduction. Keep warm.

3. Fill a medium-size saucepan with water, approximately 5 inches deep, and add the juice of 1 lemon (this will help the eggs coagulate).

4. One at a time, break the eggs into simmering water, trying to keep them separate as much as possible. Poach them for 3 minutes.

5. While the eggs are poaching, toast English muffins under a preheated broiler. Put two slices of smoked salmon on each toasted muffin half.

6. Using a slotted spoon, remove the eggs as soon as they are firm. Drain well and place one on top of each muffin half, allowing two per portion, on warm serving plates.

7. Coat each egg with béarnaise sauce, garnish with watercress, and serve at once.

SERVES 4

AVOCADO OMELETTE, SANTA BARBARA STYLE

||||||||||||||||||||||||||||||||||||||||||||||||||||||||||||||||||||||||||||||||||||||||||||||||||||||||||||||||||||||||||||||||||||||||

T his dish was inspired by the avocados of Santa Barbara, California, which are among the best in the country.

¾ cup red ripe tomatoes, peeled, seeded, and cut into ½-inch dice

¾ cup ripe avocado, peeled, pitted, and cut into ½-inch dice

10 black California jumbo olives (pitted), coarsely diced

1 cup heavy cream

Salt and freshly ground white pepper to taste

12 large eggs

8 tablespoons melted butter

1. Preheat the oven to 200°F.

2. In a large saucepan, combine tomatoes, avocado, olives, and cream. Simmer over medium high heat for 5 to 7 minutes, or until mixture thickens. Season with salt and pepper, and keep warm.

3. Using four small mixing bowls, break three eggs into each, and beat well with a fork.

4. For each omelette, heat 2 tablespoons butter in an omelette pan. When the butter is very hot, pour in eggs and stir over medium high heat until they begin to set.

8. Spoon a portion of filling mixture down the center of the omelette and, using a spatula, slide the omelette up one side of the pan and fold it over on itself. Carefully slip the folded omelette out onto a warm serving dish.

9. Garnish by spooning a portion of filling mixture along both sides of the omelette. Serve at once. Make the remaining three omelettes as quickly as possible.

4 OMELETTES

TOASTED TARTAR STEAK, LIGHTLY CURRIED

||||||||||||||||||||||||||||||||||||||||||||||||||||||||||||||||||||||||||||||||||||||||||||||||||||||||||||||||||||||

Y̸ou can invent relishes and garnishes for this dish. We use a tablespoon each of diced tomatoes, minced onion, and capers. They are served in little cups made of onion layers. You can also serve relishes in hollowed-out lemon halves.

    3 egg yolks, lightly beaten
 1 1/2 tablespoons high-quality curry powder
   1/4 cup Dijon mustard
    2 ounces anchovy fillets, drained and coarsely
        chopped
   1/4 cup capers (small size), rinsed and drained
   1/4 cup finely chopped Bermuda onion
   1/2 cup toasted pine nuts
   1/4 teaspoon freshly ground black pepper
   24 ounces freshly ground lean sirloin steak
    2 tablespoons vegetable oil

1. Combine egg yolks, curry powder, and mustard in a large mixing bowl and blend well. Add anchovies, capers, onions, pine nuts, and pepper, and mix together.

2. Add ground sirloin to mixing bowl and thoroughly combine all ingredients. Do not overmix. Adjust seasoning to taste, using more curry powder or pepper. Divide mixture into four portions, and form each portion into an oval patty.

3. Heat oil in a large frying pan until it is very hot and begins to swirl in the pan. Carefully place each patty in the hot oil. Quickly sear patties over high heat, just long enough to brown—no more than one minute on each side. Immediately remove patties from pan, and drain on paper towels to absorb excess fat. Serve at once.

SERVES 4

FRESH SALMON TARTAR, CAFÉ DES ARTISTES

||||||||||||||||||||||||||||||||||||||||||||||||||||||||||||||||||||||||||||||||||||||||||||||||||||||

1 egg yolk

2 tablespoons olive oil

1 tablespoon Dijon mustard

4 tablespoons finely diced onion

1 tablespoon finely chopped dill

1 teaspoon A-1 Sauce

   Pinch of salt

   Pinch of freshly ground white pepper

1 tablespoon fresh lemon juice

¾ pound fresh salmon fillet, skin and bones removed, coarsely and evenly chopped

2 large ripe avocados, cut in half with pits removed

4 teaspoons golden caviar

4 sprigs of dill

1. In a medium-size mixing bowl, combine egg yolk, olive oil, mustard, onion, and dill, and blend well. Season with A-1 Sauce, salt, pepper, and lemon juice.

2. Add chopped salmon, being careful not to overwork, or mixture will break down.

3. Divide tartar into four portions, and mound each into the cavity of an avocado. Place a teaspoon of caviar on top of each mound, garnish with a sprig of dill, and serve.

SERVES 4

DESSERTS

ILONA TORTE

I created and named this dish after my mother and daughter in 1969, and it is included in my *Cuisine of Hungary* (Atheneum, 1971 and 1982). One slice of it will bring temporary happiness, which is more than we get from most things these days. According to fairly reliable sources, it also acts as an aphrodisiac, and quantities of the Ilona torte will turn a puny creature into Casanova or a woman you wouldn't notice on a desert island into Madame du Barry—both of whom, by the way, indulged in quantities of chocolate.

    5 ounces semisweet chocolate, cut into small
      pieces
    1 cup sugar
    6 tablespoons unsalted butter
    8 eggs, separated
 1¾ cups plus ⅓ cup coarsely ground walnuts
    2 tablespoons fresh white-bread crumbs
      Pinch of salt
      Butter
      Flour
      Mocha Buttercream (recipe follows)

GARNISH:

    Walnut halves

1. Preheat the oven to 375°F.

2. In a medium-size saucepan, combine chocolate and sugar with ¼ cup water and cook over moderate heat for about 5 minutes, stirring occasionally until mixture is smooth. Let mixture cool for 15 minutes.

3. In a mixing bowl, beat butter until light and fluffy.

4. Add egg yolks, one at a time, beating until each is incorporated.

5. Slowly beat in chocolate syrup until well blended. Then add 1¾ cups ground walnuts and bread crumbs, mixing just enough to combine thoroughly.

6. In a large mixing bowl, whip egg whites and salt until stiff peaks form.

7. Very gently, fold egg whites into the chocolate mixture.

8. Lightly butter a 10-inch torte pan 3 inches deep. Sprinkle with flour, and shake out any excess.

9. Pour batter into pan and bake for 35 to 40 minutes. Let the cake cool in the pan for 15 minutes.

10. Invert torte onto a cooling rack, and let torte cool completely.

11. Cut the cooled torte into two layers.

12. Place top half, topside down, on a round platter.

13. Cover the cake with ¾ cup of mocha buttercream, reserving 1 cup for decoration.

14. Place the second layer on top of the filling, smooth side up.

15. Cover the top and sides of the cake with the remaining buttercream, using a flexible cake spatula.

||||||||||||||||||||||||||||||||||||||||||||||||||||||||||||||||||||||||||||||||||||||||||||||||||||||||||||||||||||||||||||||||||

16. Press the remaining ⅓ cup ground walnuts into the butter-cream on the sides of the cake.

17. Using a pastry bag with a star tip, decorate the top edges and base of the cake with the reserved 1 cup buttercream.

18. Garnish the top with walnut halves.

MOCHA BUTTERCREAM

   6 *ounces semisweet chocolate, cut into small pieces*
   2 *teaspoons instant espresso powder*
   1 *cup plus 2 tablespoons unsalted butter, at room temperature*
   3 *egg yolks*
 ⅔ *cup confectioners' sugar*

1. In a small saucepan, combine chocolate, ⅓ cup water, and espresso powder.

2. Stir over low heat until the chocolate is completely melted. Scrape into a bowl and let cool completely.

3. Using an electric mixer, cream butter until light and fluffy.

4. Add egg yolks, one at a time, beating until each is incorporated.

5. Gradually add confectioners' sugar.

6. Scrape in chocolate mixture and blend thoroughly.

SERVES 12 OR MORE

BUTTERMILK PIE

||||||||||||||||||||||||||||||||||||||||||||||||||||||||||||||||||||||||||||||||||||||||||||||||||||||||||||||||||||||||||||||

By some inexplicable transformation, this late-eighteenth-century American pie will taste almost like a lemon cheese-cake by the next day. The filling has only five simple ingredients, so it's rather difficult to explain why this pie affords such a feeling of sensuous luxury.

DOUGH

1 1/4 cups all-purpose flour

1/4 teaspoon salt

6 tablespoons very cold unsalted butter, cut into 6 pieces

2 tablespoons solid vegetable shortening

3 tablespoons ice-cold water

FILLING

3 large eggs

1 cup granulated sugar

2 cups buttermilk

1 tablespoon fresh lemon juice

1 teaspoon vanilla extract

1. Sift flour, combine with salt, and put in the bowl of a food processor fitted with a metal chopping blade. Whirl for a few seconds to mix.

2. Sprinkle butter and shortening on top of flour. Process with pulsing action for about 10 seconds, until mixture resembles coarse oatmeal.

3. Sprinkle water over mixture. Process with pulsing action for about 10 seconds, until mixture just begins to stick together, but before a ball forms.

4. Shape dough into a ball, wrap in wax paper, and chill for one hour.

5. Preheat the oven to 450°F.

6. Roll out the dough between sheets of lightly floured wax paper and then set into a 9-inch pie plate. Trim edges and crimp to form a decorative edge. Chill until firm.

7. Set a square of wax paper inside the pie shell and fill with raw beans, rice, or pie weights.

8. Bake 10 to 12 minutes, until the dough looks set. Remove beans and wax paper.

9. Prick the dough with a fork, then continue baking for 10 minutes longer, until baked through.

10. Reduce the oven temperature to 350°F.

11. In a large bowl beat eggs. Beat in sugar, then add buttermilk, lemon juice, and vanilla and mix well. Pour into baked shell.

12. Bake 50 to 60 minutes, until filling is firm and a knife inserted in the center comes out clean.

13. Serve slightly chilled, with whipped cream on the side.

SERVES 8

RYE BREAD TORTE

|||||||||||||||||||||||||||||||||||||||||||||||||||||||||||||||||||||||||||||||||||||||||||||||||||||||||||||||||||||||||||||||||||||||||||||||||||||||

This cake has culinary roots in the nineteenth century, when, in order to intensify flavors, black bread was used as an ingredient for ice cream and rye flour for cakes. It should be assembled 3 to 4 hours before serving—no sooner, or it will become soggy.

1 cup rye-bread crumbs made from crustless,
    seedless bread
1 cup ground or very finely chopped walnuts
1 teaspoon baking powder
6 large eggs, separated
    Dash of salt
1 cup granulated sugar
2 cups heavy cream
1 teaspoon powdered cinnamon
1 teaspoon vanilla extract
¾ cup raspberry jam

1. Preheat the oven to 375°F.

2. Butter the bottoms (not the sides) of three 9-inch round cake pans with removable bottoms or three 9-inch springform pans.

3. Combine bread crumbs, walnuts, and baking powder.

4. Lightly beat egg yolks.

5. Beat egg whites with salt until soft peaks form. Gradually add sugar and beat until stiff peaks form.

6. Fold one-quarter of the egg white mixture into egg yolks. Gradually fold in crumb mixture. Gently fold in remaining egg white mixture.

7. Divide the mixture evenly among the cake pans, lightly smoothing the batter with a spatula. Bake for 30 minutes, until layers are golden and pull away from pan sides in spots.

8. Run a knife around inside of pan to loosen cake from sides. Let layers cool 10 minutes in the pans on wire racks. Run a knife between cake layers and pan bottoms, and then invert each onto a rack and carefully peel the cake away from the pan bottom. Layers are soft and delicate, and should be handled gently. Let cool completely.

9. Whip cream with cinnamon and vanilla until stiff. Set aside ⅓ cup.

10. To assemble torte, spread half the whipped cream on the top of one cake layer. Cover with the second cake layer and spread with all but 1 tablespoon of the jam. Place the third cake layer on top and spread with remaining whipped cream.

11. To decorate the cake, make a spoke pattern in cream using the blunt edge of a knife. Pipe a decorative 2-inch circle in the center of the cake with the reserved ⅓ cup cream. Fill in the circle with the reserved 1 tablespoon jam.

SERVES 8 TO 12

ORANGE SAVARIN

||||||||||||||||||||||||||||||||||||||||||||||||||||||||||||||||||||||||||||||||||||||||||||||||||||||||||||||||||||||||

L eftover savarin should be sliced and toasted in a broiler, a perfect accompaniment for an afternoon tea. Credit should go to chef Michael Picciano, whose original formula was the base for our recipe. The creator of a new dish, just like the discoverer of an island, has the privilege of naming it. Stanislaus Leszczynski, king of Poland from 1704 to 1709, was an amateur baker who named his new dessert "Ali Baba," after a character in his favorite book, *A Thousand and One Nights* (or *The Arabian Nights' Entertainment*). The famous Parisian maître pâtissier, Julienne, changed the recipe slightly and renamed it "Savarin," after the famous French gastronome Brillat-Savarin.

1 ½ cups unsalted butter, at room temperature
2 ¼ cups granulated sugar
8 large eggs, separated
2 ¼ teaspoons vanilla extract
Grated rind of 2 oranges (about 1 ¼ tablespoons)
2 ¼ cups sifted all-purpose flour
¼ teaspoon baking soda
Strained juice of 2 oranges (about ½ cup)
1 ½ teaspoons cream of tartar
¼ teaspoon salt
2 to 3 tablespoons orange-flavored liqueur (optional)

1. Preheat the oven to 325°F.

2. Butter and flour a ten-inch tube pan with a removable bottom.

3. Cream butter in the large bowl of an electric mixer until fluffy. Gradually add 1¼ cups of the sugar; beat butter and sugar together until light and fluffy, about 3 minutes.

4. Add egg yolks, one at a time, beating well after each addition. Add vanilla and orange rind and beat mixture at medium speed for 5 minutes, or until light and fluffy.

5. Sift flour and baking soda together. Add to creamed mixture in three additions, alternating with orange juice and beginning and ending with dry ingredients. Beat until smooth.

6. In another large bowl beat egg whites with cream of tartar and salt until soft peaks form. Gradually add the remaining 1 cup sugar and beat at high speed until stiff peaks form. Gently fold into batter.

7. Pour batter into tube pan. Bake in the center of oven for 1 hour and 35 minutes, until the cake is golden and pulls away from the sides of the pan.

8. Remove cake pan to a wire rack. While the cake is still hot, brush with liqueur. Let cool 10 minutes, then remove from pan.

9. To serve, cut into 1-inch slices.

SERVES 18

FROZEN LEMON SOUFFLÉ

||||||||||||||||||||||||||||||||||||||||||||||||||||||||||||||||||||||||||||||||||||||||||||||||||||||||

2 *eggs, separated*
7 *tablespoons granulated sugar*
Juice and grated rind (yellow part only) of 2 lemons
1 *cup heavy cream*

GARNISH:
  Grated lemon rind
4 *fresh mint leaves*

1. Prepare four individual 4-ounce ramekins by first cutting collars out of parchment or wax paper, each 1½ inches by 10 inches. Wrap a collar around each ramekin and secure tightly with tape.

2. In a large bowl, beat egg yolks with 3 tablespoons sugar until mixture is thick and lemony in color. Add lemon juice and grated rind and continue to beat until mixture is smooth and creamy.

3. Whip cream with 2 tablespoons sugar until stiff and fold into beaten egg yolk mixture.

4. Beat egg whites until soft peaks form, and continue to beat, gradually adding the remaining 2 tablespoons sugar, until smooth and glossy and stiff. Add to whipped cream mixture and fold together very gently with a rubber scraper; be careful not to overwork, or the mixture will break down.

5. Fold mixture into the prepared ramekins, 1 inch above the rim. Put in the freezer for at least 2 hours.

6. A half hour before serving, remove soufflés from the freezer to the refrigerator.

7. When ready to serve, remove paper collars. Garnish the top of the soufflés with grated lemon rind and mint leaves. Serve at once.

4 SOUFFLÉS

CASSIS AND BEAUJOLAIS SHERBET

When Nero wearied of playing "Turkey in the Straw" on his fiddle, he concocted a mixture of "honey, fruit pulp, and wine" and poured it over snow that had been brought from the top of a mountain by fleet-footed runners. Since that time, every self-respecting hedonist has tried to capture the frozen taste of wine or fruit, and the Café has developed a daily changing sherbet. This one is ideal when no ripe fruit is available.

1 bottle (750 ml) red Beaujolais wine
1 cup sugar
¼ cup cassis
   Juice of 2 lemons
   Juice of 1 orange

1. In a medium saucepan, combine wine and sugar and cook over medium high heat until reduced to 2 cups; remove from heat. Stir in cassis and lemon and orange juice. Refrigerate until cold.

2. Process in an ice cream maker according to the manufacturer's directions. (If ice cream maker is not available, pour mixture into a large shallow pan and place in freezer. While mixture is freezing, stir frequently with a fork to break up ice crystals and lumps.)

3. To serve, spoon into balloon-shaped wineglasses.

MAKES APPROXIMATELY 1 PINT